Copyright © 2022 Lawrence Winston

All rights reserved. Printed in the United States of America. No part of this book may be used or reproduced in any manner whatsoever without written permission except in the case of brief quotations in critical articles or reviews.

Cover Design: Jeremiah Dean
Typesetting, Book Layout by
Enger Lanier Taylor for In Due Season Publishing

Published By: In Due Season Publishing ®
Huntsville, Alabama
indueseasonpublishing@gmail.com
www.indueseasonpublishing.com

ISBN-13: 978-1-970057-20-1
ISBN-10: 1-970057-20-3

TABLE OF CONTENTS

- Words of Encouragement
- Acknowledgments
- Introduction
- Day # 1 - What to Expect
- Day # 2 - Strength
- Day # 3 - Spontaneous
- Day # 4 - Supernatural Acceleration
- Day # 5 - Rain
- Day # 6 - Days of Awe
- Day # 7 - Blessings Pt 1.
- Day # 7.2 - Blessings Pt 2.
- Day # 8 - Blueprint and Instructions
- Day # 9 - Rest
- Day # 10 - New Launch
- Day # 11 - Placement
- Day # 12 - Renewed Strength
- Day # 13 - Self Control
- Day # 14 - Decrees for Unburden

- Day # 15 - Be Bold in Prayer
- Day # 16 - Open Doors
- Day # 17 - Sow
- Day # 18 - Great Things Are on the Horizon
- Day # 19 - Breakthrough
- Day # 20 - The Path
- Day # 21 - Dwell
- Testimony

To My Spiritual Son,
Prophet Lawrence "Nate" Winston,

It is with such great honor that I am graced with the opportunity to encourage you on this awesome momentous occasion. I have watched you grow over the years, and I must say that God has done an excellent job with you. I'm so excited because I can see the shift! I believe that this breakthrough is a breakthrough that you have never even seen before, it never even hit you that it was going to happen in such a way as this, and I'm just happy that I can encourage you to press on because this is just the beginning!

On behalf of myself and the Late Great Chief Apostle Darrell Roberts Sr., I'm writing with a glad heart to congratulate you on launching your new book. I can only imagine the excitement you must feel right now over God's blessing. I trust that you are aware that not only will you reap the benefits of being a blessing to the Kingdom of God, but everyone that reads this book will reap from your God-given strength and courage that have guided you with each step taken towards achieving this goal. Be mindful of the message Jesus gave us, that He is "the vine, ye are the branches. He that abideth in me, and I in him, the same bringeth forth much fruit: for without me ye can do nothing" (John 15:5).

When we trust in and listen to Him, He will do the same and help us to achieve with Him what we could never do alone. Therefore, a book founded on the values of Jesus can be successful for you and the entire Kingdom. Your family here at Deliverance & Victory Five-Fold Worship Ministries wants only to see you do well and do God's work. This is a joyous occasion where we can come together and celebrate you.

Remember that you are blessed, and with Jesus Christ in your life, there is nothing that you cannot achieve. While on this journey, there may be moments of trepidation, but you will also experience times of excitement about the future God holds for you and your family as you embark upon this great venture. I trust that you will continue to keep God first in your life as you begin your new journey.

The Bible gives us a very important word in Matthew 6:33 that you probably have heard repeatedly: "But seek ye first the kingdom of God and his righteousness, and all these things will be added unto you." The promises of God are just that; promises. Someone once said the following about God's Promises; "God makes a promise; faith believes it, hope anticipates it, patience quietly awaits it." Harry Truman said, "I found that the men and women who got to the top were those who did the jobs they had in hand, with everything they had of energy and enthusiasm and hard work."

It is true that when we think about quality and not quantity, the second half of that equation often falls in line. We also realize that God is the ultimate rewarder of the efforts of men, and He is the one who exalts and promotes. *1 Peter 5:6 – Humble yourselves, therefore, under God's mighty hand, that he may lift you up in due time.* THIS IS YOUR TIME, PROPHET!!! The Bible also tells us that we should do everything as if we are doing it for God Himself. *1 Cor. 10:31 – So whether you eat or drink or whatever you do, do it all for the glory of God.*

You have worked hard and have been rightfully recognized and rewarded for your efforts. You are to be commended, and I encourage you to continue to do your work to the Glory of God, and you will be amazed at how the favor of God will rest on your life. REST IN YOUR GOSHEN SEASON!

May the Lord God Bless you with His mighty hand of provision.

Chief Apostle Vera Roberts
Deliverance & Victory Fivefold Worship Center
Michigan City, Indiana

Author Lawrence Winston is one of my favorite people in the entire world. He reminds me of an iceberg by showing you humility, restraint, and quietness on the surface. However, the deeper look beneath the surface reveals the massive internal structures that power this man of great character, strength, and ultimate faith in all things God. His writings come from a place of credibility, and you can sense his authentic relationship with God birthed from the reality of who he truly is. There is no hypocritical distance in Lawrence Winston. What he proclaims and who he actually is are refreshingly the same. This mature place that he has journeyed to in his walk with the Lord gives him clear sight and wisdom to unpack the mind of God. Lawrence delivers divine discoveries throughout each chapter that will trigger inner transactions with our God. You will be blessed by what you have in your hands. May this book assist you in knowing God in the generation you serve.

Apostle Dion Campbell

Press Towards Your Call

Brethren, I count not myself to have apprehended: but this one thing I do, forgetting those things which are behind, and reaching forth unto those things which are before, I press toward the mark for the prize of the high calling of God in Christ Jesus (Philippians 3:13-14).

While traveling back to St. Louis from my family reunion in Kansas City, I talked with my cousin about my dad and the impact he made while pastoring the church we grew up in, Bethel Temple Church of Christ Holiness USA. He accepted his call to pastor, even when it didn't seem like it was the right time. After dropping her off at her house, I began talking to the Lord about how I saw the pieces coming together in my life prophetically. Well, at that moment, I chose to lay hold fully of what Christ Jesus laid hold of me for. God has a higher calling for all of us, but sometimes we struggle with the who, what, when, where, and how method. He gives us a glimpse of what He wants us to do, but after seeing it, we immediately focus on what seems to be the barriers in front of us. Paul is speaking to the church of Philippi about pressing toward the mark. He shares how important it is not to get caught up in what you know and forgetting the things which are behind. However, the most powerful thing he encourages the church to do is to reach for what is before them and press toward the mark.

Listen, thoughts will come to get you to reject or doubt what God has spoken over your life. You must decide that no matter what, even though you may not see the full picture or are not quite sure how all of this will pass, you will reach towards what is before you and press towards your call. Don't second guess yourself! Keep moving toward your call; God will reveal even more to you before you least expect it. I learned from my father's story that he realized by Holy Spirit that the call on his life was not just for him but for others as well. People are waiting for you to accept and walk in the call of God for your life.

Words of encouragement by:

Apostle Pruitt
New Wind International St, Louis MO

Acknowledgments

Glory Be to God. Without Him, none of this would have been possible.

To my beautiful wife, Mrs. Winston, who always inspires me to continue to strive for greatness. I thank you for being a voice that keeps me grounded, calm, levelheaded, focused, and humble. You are the definition of a Proverbs 31 woman, and I am honored to have you in my life. I'm in love with you as you opened my eyes on my way to my breakthrough and encouraged me along the way to conquer what was before me. You cultivate and nurture our children in love, which is key to the home environment that stimulates growth and healing. I thank you for all that you do, day in and day out. It may seem as if it goes unnoticed, but I want to thank you and let you know how grateful I am.

To my beautiful mother, Rubie Adams, thank you. I've watched you, and you have a story that needs to be told. Seeing you overcome so many things in your life and your strength to go through and continue to move forward is amazing to me. I said this often that it's something about this George family that resembles strength. It's good to know that I am from a tribe of strength. Thank you for being you.

My amazing mother-in-law, Annette Bryant, thank you for helping my wife and me daily. We have a unique lifestyle, and many will not understand that, but I'm grateful you are a part of it. You've been a consistent help from day one. The Winston family loves you.

My Apostles Darrell and Vera Roberts, you two came into my life at a pivotal time when I needed a spiritual lifeguard to rescue me. You took my wife and me in and groomed us through the good, the bad, and the ugly. You taught us spiritual principles, and how to apply them, as well as showed us how to be living vessels. I'm honored to have such great leaders' teachings and spiritual impartation. Apostle V prophesied to my wife and me in 2012 at a critical time in our life. She said, "We had several books to write, and people were waiting on us." That prophetic word gave us hope, which still carries weight today. Apostle Darrell, thank you for your words of wisdom, passion, and love for God. Thank you for sharing your testimonies with us and never holding back about the victories that God brought you through. You were indeed a walking miracle. I am forever grateful to know and to witness God do great things in your life. Apostle, you set the bar high. You are a man skilled in many things, but what stood out the most was how much you loved your wife and your willingness to be made whole again. You've always said that you were marred in the potter's hand. Thank you for allowing me to be your spiritual son. Love you, Apostle D.

Apostle Dion Campbell, my mentor, I'm grateful to have you as a mentor and friend. I've always received wise counsel from you. You are a solid individual who isn't afraid to tell me when I am wrong and always encourages me to do the right things and make the best decisions. You really pushed me to understand my spiritual identity and who God has called me to be. The man-touring mentorship program for men launched prophetically before the world was shifting into what we see it as now. The importance of being in position as men sharpened our spiritual antennas and challenged us. As I look back, our meetings were very prophetic and intense. Thank you for being very instrumental during my time of breakthrough.

Apostle Pruitt, you are a true friend to my wife and me. Your love for God's people is genuine. You came into our lives when we were searching for an answer from God. The profound, prophetic word you spoke into my life shifted my faith during a critical time. I'm grateful for "The Safe Place Group," and the strong leaders my wife and I are connected to. Your love for God is a light and is organic. The Covering Prayer Line for men launched during my journey to my breakthrough. I'm so grateful for that organization. Thank you all so much you.

Brenda Cates, thank you for stepping in and making a huge impact on the Winston's life. You have a heart of gold, and we value that about you. You truly are a gift and a blessing to many. Thank you for your continuous support.

Special Thanks

I want to take the time to thank everyone, and please forgive me if I didn't mention everyone. I'm grateful to have the invitation to sit down and document events where God has stepped in time and time again in my and my family's life. Shout out to my church family, Deliverance & Victory Fivefold Worship Ministry, and the KCCFI family. Shout out to my English teacher Ms. Lori Wilson-Patterson who encouraged me to continue to write. She recognized that I loved writing and encouraged me to pursue it. Those college days were tough, but Ms. Lori motivated me.

A special shout-out to my writing coach, Sophia Ruffin. She is amazing. She pushed me into birthing this out and completing this book. She really stirred us up in class and supplied us with the resources and tools to *go forward*. I went through a five-week intense writing course in her Ready Writer's program, and it was worth it. Thank you to all the instructors that were connected to the program. I'm grateful to be a part of a supportive team that helped bring this book to life.

21-Day Divine Breakthrough Experience

INTRODUCTION

This journey is full of experiences I recorded while fasting and seeking the Lord. I'm praying that this manual will become the GPS to help unlock your breakthrough and position you for your next. While fasting and praying, I experienced a divine season of acceleration that shifted my journey to pursue God in a new way. Hidden things were revealed, prayers were answered, and revelation was downloaded with purpose highlighted when I responded to the call.

My wife and I experienced angelic help, and supernatural downloads poured into our household throughout this journey. The key is making it intentional to get before the Lord. God began to minister to me in ways I couldn't have ever imagined. God is real, and His Word is true. Dedicating time to receive fresh manna and hearing from God became a daily routine. That intimate space alone was priceless. It doesn't matter if it's fifteen minutes, thirty minutes, or even an hour. God began to give me a new thirst and desire I've yearned for, and I'm grateful. God's timing revealed new assignments and relationships that were to come, doors that would open, and victories sealed on our behalf.

Believe and allow God to take you to places you've never been before, spiritually and physically. New gifts you didn't ask for will be given to you because of His purpose and plans.

Frequently I examine myself, knowing what God delivered me out of and how he saved my life. It's a constant reminder to never allow myself to be entangled in bondage again. Understanding that He first loved me is a crucial component to pursue and to be grateful for, and now I can walk in liberty.

Words of Encouragement

Raise your level of expectation and take the limits off God and dare to believe for greater things to happen in your life. Begin to walk out onto the water and be strong in your faith. His love is vast and deep. It's unsearchable for what He has done and what He's about to do in your life. The scripture says, exceeding, abundantly above all that we can ask or think (Ephesians 3:20). I declare that over your life today. The question is, are you ready to take the steps toward your breakthrough?

"Then said he unto me, Fear not, Daniel: for from the first day that thou didst set thine heart to understand, and to chasten thyself before thy God, thy words were heard, and I am come for thy words." Daniel 10:12

Day 1

What to Expect

- A new realm of glory
- God's love is rich; it's undeniable
- New ground and new territory
- Open doors
- God is positioning you.
- Elohim

What does breakthrough look like? What are the steps to getting a breakthrough? Well, I'm glad that you have this prayer journal in your hand as a point of contact. In this journal, you'll find testimonies and divine encounters that will help you identify your path to your breakthrough.

Walk Out Onto the Water

Experience God in a new perspective and in a new way. I want to encourage you and testify that God is going to bring you through. Even in your darkest times, God never lost sight of you. He will speak to your situation and shift you forward in your faith. God said He would never leave us nor forsake us. We don't know what the next chapter of our lives will look like as believers.

Nevertheless, by faith, we must continue to move forward and trust God's timing. I'm praying that God will position you spiritually, mentally, physically, and financially to move the Kingdom forward and that your faith will be pleasing to Him. I'm thanking God for a fresh pour and a fresh anointing that shall fall fresh on you. I prophesy that you are the new wine equipped for this hour of breakthrough that shall be seen because the glory of God is upon you. Your biggest assignment will be striving to be a better you every day.

I Declare

If the Son therefore shall make you free, ye
Shall be free indeed.
John 8:36

Let go of the things from the past that meant your future no good and walk in freedom.

Victory Awaits You.

The Importance of Spending Time with the Father

I encourage you to get before God and hear from Him daily. Intimate time with God is priceless. The alone time with Him is refreshing and helps you with decision-making for the day. Intimate time with the Lord reveals the real you and the areas you need to work on. I love that about God because He doesn't expose us in the areas where we have fallen short. But He covers us in love and gives us the grace to get things right.

Instructions During Prayer

God will begin to speak and show you the new things to come as you launch out into the deep even more. In my prayer time, I've experienced God positioning me ahead of situations and give me insight. Your discernment level will increase as you spend time with the Heavenly Father. It's a crucial part of your discipleship of following Christ and a key to your breakthrough.

Breakthrough Decree:

I decree that the seed I have been cultivating shall grow and be fruitful and multiply in Jesus' mighty name.

But as it is written, Eye hath not seen, nor ear heard, neither have entered into the heart of man, the things which God hath prepared for them that love him.
1 Corinthians 2:9 9

Day 2

Strength

- Renewed strength
- Where we are weak, God is strong
- 2 Corinthians 12: 9-11
- Matthew 4:4
- God has ordained you to be in a specific place at a certain time.
- Fresh wind - the Ruach
- Seeing miracles arise
- Open doors no man can shut Revelation 3:8
- Suddenly moments

Continue to Pray for Strength

We often grow tired of particular situations and become impatient in everyday circumstances. I want to encourage you that where we are weak is where God is strong in our lives. We often overlook the steps that God wants us to master. We need to slow down and hear God during these times. Trying to rush out of what He allowed in our lives to happen can cause us to miss the very thing that God wants us to focus on. God is developing your character and building your integrity if we allow Him to lead. The steps of breakthrough are not only for you, but they are for others as well. Someone will need your testimony to help them overcome what they are facing. *Don't skip the steps. I repeat, do not skip the steps.* God has predestined and ordained you to be in a particular place at a certain time, so use it wisely to be a good steward. This fresh chapter in your life is called *again*. I declare that for you. You can begin to write again. You can create again. You can sing again because the joy of the Lord is your strength. Just ask the Lord to do it again. I declare a fresh wind; *the Ruach* of God will usher you into that new place. Get acquainted with the many names of God so that you may identify Him in *all things* and begin to declare His name in the atmosphere. As you learn His characteristics, you will become stronger in your journey.

New Excitement

New adventures, new ideas, new creations, and new expectations will begin to flow, and this will increase your faith. We call this the stretching of our faith, which will develop maturity and growth. Sometimes you get uncomfortable, but know that God is elevating you and building characteristics in your life. Allow God to restore what was lost - your joy, strength, admiration, and your gratitude. You can access peace, and it all begins with a yes. Saying yes to God's will and His way will lift the burdens of life off your shoulders, and you will see the newness that He has in store for you (Jeremiah 29:11).

Walking Upright Before the Lord

Walking upright before the Lord is so dope, and it comes with so many benefits. Listen. We must break that "get it out the mud mentality" Psalms 84:11 says For the Lord God is a sun and shield: the Lord will give grace and glory: no good thing will he withhold from them that walk uprightly. We don't realize that we are our own hindrance from accessing the fullness of what God wants us to have. And it's not always the material blessings that will come, but some of the best blessings that came to me were spiritual gifts and things I didn't even deserve. God saw it fit for me to have them, and I can tell you today that I am grateful for those types of gifts because it lets me know that God loves me and I'm on the right track.

Breakthrough Decrees:

I decree new doors will open for me.

I decree that my career will be blessed.

I decree that I will see miracles, signs, and wonders.

I decree that God's Word will not return to Him void.

I decree a quick help.

I decree that a suddenly happens in my life.

I decree financial increase.

I decree a spiritual awakening.

Day 3

Spontaneous

- Miraculous
- Prayer
- Tongues
- Strong and mighty
- A new path
- A new journey
- A new destination

Great and Mighty Things in This Season

Be encouraged and thank God for today. God is calling you higher. There is a calling on your life, and he wants to reveal it to you.

Having an Elevated Mindset

Continue to spend time in prayer and your holy language. The more that you do it, it becomes natural. During my prayer time, I always try to tap into a high point that launches me into my holy language. It's not something that's practiced or planned; it flows naturally. It's a frequency that aligns your ability to hear, and God will begin to show and tell you things. I would also encourage you to get an actual notebook and record what God is saying and revealing. So many ideas can be birthed out in prayer.

Spontaneous

Watch for God to do things above your understanding. The Bible tells us in *James 1:17, Every good and perfect gift is from above, coming down from the Father of the Heavenly lights, who does not change like shifting shadows.* Keep in mind that you are packed with purpose on purpose. If God has not changed His thoughts about you and toward you, why are you doubting and self-sabotaging yourself? I decree that rivers of living water will flow out of you. Don't be afraid of the spontaneous moves God is making for you in this season.

New Path & New Journey

Come up higher. Let God give you a bird's eye view of your new path. Learning how to pray and prepare is an essential key to your breakthrough. So often, we find ourselves in a place of "trying to figure things out." I want to encourage you with *Psalms 119:105, Thy word is a lamp unto my feet, and a light unto my path.* Meaning you will know and visibly see the path God has designed for you.

Breakthrough Decree:

I decree that doors are opening for me.

Favor is locating me in this season.

I decree that I am encountering God in a new way.

A new sound shall come forth out of my prayer.

Words of Encouragement

Allow God to correct you. He chastises those He loves, so it's only right to receive His correction as well. Not only will it make you stronger it's also building character and integrity.

This will open the ability to love and see from a new perspective.

For whom the Lord loveth he chasteneth, and scourgeth every son whom he receiveth. 7 If ye endure chastening, God dealeth with you as with sons; for what son is he whom the father chasteneth not?
Hebrews 12:6-7 6

**So, reap the benefits
of enduring and being called a son.**

Day 4

Supernatural Acceleration

- Elevation
- Miracles, Signs & Wonders
- God's hand is strong
- Revelation & Knowledge
- Glory Carriers
- The Oil & The Presence
- Awakening

Stay focused. With everyday activities in our lives, we must develop the ability to hear God's voice even when the world around us is loud. God does things beyond our understanding and sight. As you begin to study more and spend time with God, you will find that He still speaks in the simplest ways. Covid 19 was something we couldn't physically see, but it made a huge impact on the world and it was loud. It's crazy just thinking how a virus could be so loud. It changed our very way of living, communicating, and traveling. It made us aware of the unseen and taught us how to gird up even more. It also ushered us into a deeper prayer life and communion with God.

God did not cause the pandemic, but I believe that He allowed it so that He could get us to a place of spiritual awareness and center our focus and attention back on Him. The Bible says in *Isaiah 55:8-9 8 For my thoughts are not your thoughts, neither are your ways my ways, saith the Lord. 9 For as the heavens are higher than the earth, so are my ways higher than your ways, and my thoughts than your thoughts.*

This acceleration will be both physical and spiritual for the body of Christ. Unseen and unheard-of types of blessings will usher us into a new place. Even your spiritual gifts are going to go to another dimension. God doesn't want us to be caught off guard by the enemy's tactics and devices. In Hosea 4:6, it tells us that we perish because of the lack of knowledge because we choose to reject it. Men and women of God, I urge you to stay focused on your *"God Assignment."* Seek understanding in your prayer time with God; it all has a purpose and a plan. Although everyone comes from different walks of life, I want to encourage you to hold tight to the revelation given to you. You are born for such a time as this, and this acceleration will draw others to Christ. You are important!

- ***Prophetic Word***

    Suddenly and immediately, you will begin to see rapid change. You're going to see and get more done within less time because of the acceleration of God.

- ***Prophetic Insight***

    What was meant for evil, God used it for His good which caused a supernatural acceleration. Things will happen at a rapid pace.

Elevation

Write down the gems that God will begin to give you, even your dreams and your visions. Fresh revelation and understanding are being released upon you. This revelation comes with instructions and directions that will shift and position you for your next. Divine directions and connections will assist you in the path God has laid for you. Resources will become available to you to carry out what God has spoken. The invitation to come up higher in the spirit realm will help you see how to move.

The following steps will help you develop your ability to hear God:

- Begin to journal your dreams and the things God will speak to you throughout the day.
- Some use notebooks and write them out; others use their phones for voice recordings.

Day 5

Rain

- Spontaneous Miracles
- The Good Father
- Elohim
- Jehovah Shamma "The Lord is there" Ezekiel 48:35
- Victories
- Glory Carriers
- Healing

Great & Mighty

Call unto me, and I will answer thee, and show thee great and mighty things, which thou knowest not.
Jeremiah 33:3

Leading into this prayer, God was speaking to me about rain. I'm stirred up because this whole season, I can see God leading us to the seed and the promise, so I am encouraged because when God is moving, showing us things, and speaking to us about the current season and the seasons to come, I like to call it a scavenger hunt as God is saying follow me. I can feel a shift happening that God is setting the stage and leading His people to the promise. I'm reminded of the scripture *1 Corinthians 3:6, I have planted, Apollos watered; but God gave the increase*. Anytime you see an increase, just know that God has allowed it and that He caused it to happen.

This word came to my wife and me during a time when we were faithful in our giving. This is a major key to your breakthrough: being intentional in your giving, whether it be love, time, resources, or finances. God said He would give seed to the sower (2 Corinthians 9:10). So whatever God has placed on and in you, maximize it. Your testimony and your purpose are connected to someone else's breakthrough.

I want to encourage you to get familiar with the many names of God. This will allow you to always identify him. Developing a prayer life, seeking His presence, and wanting to receive a fresh pour of his daily anointing causes a Rhema word that will fall fresh on you, and you will begin to flow in the spirit. I'm reminded of the word in *Matthew 4:4, But he answered and said, It is written, Man shall not live by bread alone, but by every word that proceedeth out of the mouth of God.* Just take a moment and think about that. That's powerful, and do not take that lightly. God has great things in store for us, but we must walk in authority. Greater works will produce miracles, signs, and wonders. Abiding in Him produces power, and you will see the manifestation of His promises. We have the power to heal, the power to speak life, the power to decree, the power for breakthrough, and the power over addictions in Jesus.

Stay Focused on the Assignment.

What is your assignment? Allow God to give you prophetic instructions for your breakthrough. In the times that we live in, we can see that God is moving quickly. When He gives you instructions, directions, or insight, begin to move in that space that He has opened for you. You're born for such a time as this. I'm reminded of the scripture *Jeremiah*

1:5 Before I formed thee in the belly I knew thee; and before thou camest forth out of the womb I sanctified thee, and I ordained thee a prophet unto the nations.

You are a glory carrier; it's time to rise higher so your eye can get sharp in the spirit realm. God is inviting you to see. He wants to give you insight. There are ideas and inventions that only you can usher into this generation because God spoke them. You are built for this! There is a fresh pour of the gifts, and I decree new growth to come forth now in Jesus' mighty name.

Day 6

Days of Awe

- The crossover
- 5782
- New time
- Dunamis Power
- Glory
- Burdens lifted
- Latter rain
- Jeremiah 29:11
- Unexpected miracles

You Crossed Over Into a New Time

Start your day by exalting God and thanking Him for the crossover into your new season. It's important that you celebrate this day. Many may not understand your journey, and no one knows what you have had to endure to get to this point in your life. There were probably times that you went through the most challenging seasons with a smile on your face. I decree that peace and calmness will be your portion. God orchestrates things on our behalf even when we don't understand or feel His presence. I want to encourage you that He is with you. I'm reminded of *Deuteronomy 31:8, "And the LORD, he it is that doth go before thee; he will be with thee, he will not fail thee, neither forsake thee: fear not, neither be dismayed."* Listen, God has gone before you to make all the rough places smooth. I know that sounds easy, but we must depend on God's Word and believe the things He has spoken out of His mouth concerning us.

A Time of Refreshing

In this season, open your eyes, begin to see the new, and watch God lift the burdens off you. Whatever the load may be, the key to seeing the fullness of this promise is to operate in faith. The scripture says in *Hebrews 11:6, But without faith it is impossible to please him: for he that cometh to God must believe that he is, and that he is a rewarder of them that diligently seek him.*

5782

What is 5782? 5782 is the start of Rosh Hashanah. In Hebrew, it marks the beginning of the year on the Jewish calendar. In 2022 it started on September 6th. 5782 came to me by just listening in my time of fasting and praying. I was listening to a well-known prophet, and he mentioned those numbers and their symbolic meaning, which then gained my attention even more and urged me to pay close attention to what was being said. Understanding the times we are living in the message unlocked so much. 5782 means awake, awaken, arouse, exulted, incite, excited, triumphant, lifted, and raised. That within itself is powerful. This prophetic foresight is direction for how your year will be, so be encouraged.

Homework Assignment:

I want to encourage you to do a deeper study into these symbolic numbers. There is more that God will unpack as you continue your journey to your breakthrough.

Words of Encouragement

In my personal breakthrough journal on day five, God had me looking at and researching the word *rain* during the seed of promise season. The rain is just an indicator of where we are headed. September 8, 2021, is when this prophecy was recorded, and it was literally raining on this day. God still speaks. We must pay attention to what He is saying. I said to the Lord, "I see you," and I'm learning His way and how He is moving.

The New Path

This is an excellent time to take a praise break because God is going to elevate you. All the things you went through were for a reason, and God is going to use those very things that caused you to be down, overlooked, and unappreciated to really minister from that place to help bring others out of bondage with your testimony. Always keep in mind that your breakthrough is a way out for others, and they need what you have and what God has placed inside of you. I just heard the word *key holder*. God said you are a key holder, and your breakthrough will set the captives free. So allow God to lead. He is the head of our life. He's the good, good Father. He has our best interest in mind. Jeremiah 29:11 says *For I know the thoughts that I think toward you, saith the Lord, thoughts of peace, and not of evil, to give you an expected end.*

- ***Prophetic Word***

    I prophesy that unexpected miracles will manifest in your life, in Jesus' Mighty Name.

    I declare that your testimony will set the captives free.

Day 7 – Part 1

Blessings

- Jehovah Nissi
- Change
- Identity
- New doors
- Asking for guidance as little children
- Trust the Father
- *Proverbs 3:5-6 5 Trust in the Lord with all your heart and lean not on your own understanding; 6 in all your ways submit to him, and he will make your paths straight.*

The Pouring

Always go into prayer empty and with a clear conscience. Throughout our busy day of caring for the family, responsibilities, etc., it's hard to find that space of silence to reflect and recharge. Yet, it's essential to have that space every day; your mental health is important. At times throughout this journal, I found myself getting up between four and six o'clock in the morning to pray, reflect and recharge. It helped set the day for me. As you develop that personal time with God, you will begin to witness a refreshing change. I've witnessed God pour fresh impartation, revelation, and new ideas into my life, and it blessed my hands and the ability to think and believe on a higher frequency.

Words cannot describe the feeling of His presence; it's priceless and feels like a breath of fresh air. *Exodus 17:15, And Moses built an altar, and called the name of it Jehovah Nissi*: I want to remind you that God is victorious and a very present help in times of trouble. He is Jehovah Nissi (The Lord is my banner). My family and I have experienced so many challenges and I can truly tell you that God has never failed us.

Trusting the Father

Your yes to God is a major key to your breakthrough. Coming into alignment with His Word is your yes. The road of discipleship isn't easy, and yes, it came with some tears and sleepless nights. But God watches over His Word to perform it. Be encouraged, continue to be patient and wait. It's important to stay in the vein abide in Him so the Word can hover over us and manifest in us so that we can not only be blessed but a blessing to others. *Being confident of this very thing, that he which hath begun a good work in you will perform it until*

the day of Jesus Christ
Philippians 1:6

Watch God Perform His Word

Keep moving forward by faith. Things that will help you breakthrough are singing, praying, and crying. Yes, it's ok to cry out. It releases toxins and chemicals in the body that could reduce stress. Dancing, going for walks, trying different things, and going to other places are important things for your mental health.

Sometimes you must have a change of scenery to see the fullness of God's promise. And it's ok if you don't understand. The Bible tells us to lean not unto our own understanding. Things will not happen overnight. But surely, as I testify, all things work together for the good of those who love the Lord. Things will eventually shift in our favor, as we begin to get an understanding that God was really building us from the inside out.

Who Does God Say You Are?

Let me remind you that you are a child of the Most High God and that you are royal. You are the seed of Abraham, Isaac, and Jacob. We are co-heirs with Christ. This is the confidence and posture you must have as you approach your breakthrough. Getting around individuals that will speak life to and over you, people that inspire you to be great, people that will lift you in prayer. One of the keys to my breakthrough was knowing that God loves me. He cares, and knowing who I am in Him gave me the confidence to move forward.

Identity

I suffered from low self-esteem after dealing with identity issues in my teenage years and through my young adulthood stage. I valued the opinions of others more than I cared for myself. No pamphlet of instructions comes with life, but don't allow that to be your excuse not to want more for yourself. Life's lessons taught me, and I thought I knew everything, but I didn't know anything. My mother explained to me as a young adult that life was just starting for me and that I should take it seriously. She never judged me on the decisions that I made. She would always say to me, "Just keep on living." I never knew what that meant until I hit bottom and couldn't see my way up or how to get out.

I felt manipulated, hurt, ashamed, and afraid. I was tired of the way I was living because I was recycling what I was taking in on others. I wanted to change. I remember crying out to God to change me, and this bright light was shining through my living room window, and I just felt like God had heard me. I felt at peace for the first time. Sometimes it takes us to hit bottom so God can deal with us in our brokenness.

> *"I cried unto God with my voice, even unto God with my voice; and he gave ear unto me."*
> ***Psalm 77:1***

Change

I was humbled and had to admit to The King of Kings that I needed Him because I had hit the bottom and couldn't see myself getting up without Him. It's something when the Heavenly Father takes you, wraps you in his arms, and begins ministering to you. All it took was for me to open my mouth and confess that I needed Him. The Father's love is a guide. Be encouraged as you continue to pursue your breakthrough. God has a plan and purpose ordained for us; we must identify the call, respond to what he has spoken, and know our identity. Be encouraged; your breakthrough is on the horizon.

<u>*Breakthrough Decree*</u>:

I will experience a refreshing experience.

I decree that I am walking boldly in Christ.

All things have become new in my life.

I am walking in the newness of God.

Day 7 – Part 2

Blessings

- El-Shaddai, "God Almighty," The God who is all-sufficient and all-bountiful,
- the source of all blessings.
- In His image and in His Likeness
- Fresh Wind
- The Breath of God
- Ruach
- Kabod

El – Shaddai: The Source Of All Blessings

Today in prayer, take time to thank God for the blessing of being created in His image and His likeness. Thank God for breathing life into you. The Ruach; and for the kabod, the glory being visible on and in us and the ability to walk in it and carry the glory with power and authority. Delight in His way and in His path. I know we frequently have a mindset that's on autopilot. But trust me, stepping out of the norm and trusting God is okay. You'll be surprised at how far He will take you.

I'm thanking God for the new dreams and visions that are about to flow into your life. I thank God for the unheard-of blessings that are about to overflow in your life, ministry, finances, and ability to create wealth. Live in the abundance and dwell in the good land.

I Decree That You Will Prosper in This Season

1 Corinthians 2:9, But as it is written, Eye hath not seen, nor ear heard, neither have entered into the heart of man, the things which God hath prepared for them that love him. Today, I decree that the unheard-of blessings will fall fresh on you today in Jesus' Mighty Name.

El-Shaddai

Thank God for being great and mighty from whom all blessings flow. We thank you, Lord, for being a strong tower and a refuge for us to dwell in.

Here are key scriptures that will navigate you on your journey.

I will instruct thee and teach thee in the way which thou shalt go. I will guide thee with mine eye. **Psalms 32:8**

Thy word is a lamp unto my feet, and a light unto my path. **Psalm 119:105**

The name of the Lord is a strong tower: the righteous runneth into it, and is safe. **Proverbs 18:10**

Create in me a clean heart, O God; and renew a right spirit within me. **Psalm 51:10**

24 The Lord bless thee, and keep thee:25 The Lord make his face shine upon thee, and be gracious unto thee:

26 The Lord lift up his countenance upon thee, and give thee peace. **Numbers 6:24-26**

Getting It Right Before Him

Now is the time that you ask God for forgiveness and thank Him for His grace and mercy. *Lord, we thank you for the pureness of the oil that you can get out of our lives. We thank you, Lord, for drawing the best out of us despite our shortcomings.* Seeing God move in our lives changes how we think and go about our daily activities. A level of gratitude and a heart of thanksgiving overtakes us. Being able to lift the name of the Lord is a blessing.

- *<u>Prophetic Word</u>*:

    God is moving you forward. God is going to release to you the blueprint and new instructions, along with new ideas that will cause you to move forward.

<u>*Breakthrough Decree*</u>:

I decree that unheard-of blessings are falling fresh on me in Jesus' Mighty Name.

I decree that the hand of the Lord protects me on all sides: The north, the south, the east, and the west.

I decree that the hand of God will block what was meant to delay me.

I decree that I will arrive to my destination on time.

Prayer

We thank you Lord that you will come and see about us. We cry out to you oh God , you are The Holy One fill this place on today God. Fill this temple, fill this tabernacle and continue to pour even the more.

Day 8

Blueprint & Instructions

- Trust God
- Revelation
- Where we are weak, God is strong
- 2 Corinthians 12:9-11
- Author and finisher of our faith
- Called & Cultivated
- A fresh pour of the anointing

Building

Lately, I've been watching DIY videos. Out of nowhere, something about them caught my eye.

Watching something broken down and turning it into something of value is interesting. All the steps and interesting tools needed for particular jobs are very prophetic to me. I knew God was speaking through the DIY videos to catch my attention because I am not handy with tools by far *(laughing)*. Let me encourage you today: God is the master builder, and there are specific tools and blueprints that He has for our lives. Often we run from it or deny that God is calling us to do a work. Many are called, but few are chosen. I can't hire a plumber to do a roofing job. They don't have the same tools, but both have the ability to build. God has equipped you with tools you must use and walk in with confidence and authority because only you are equipped to do it.

"According to the grace of God which is given unto me, as a wise masterbuilder, I have laid the foundation, and another buildeth thereon. But let every man take heed how he buildeth thereupon."
1 Corinthians 3:10

Instruction & Insight

Then he openeth the ears of men, and

sealeth their instruction.
Job 33:16

Keys

- One of the keys to our breakthrough is the ability to follow instructions. Take time today to reflect, thank God, and hear His voice. Begin to thank Him for revelation and understanding of where you are now. Glorify the Lord for every weak area that is revealed to you. The Bible says His power is made perfect in our weakness so that Christ's power may rest on us *(2 Corinthians 12:9-11)*.

- Another key to your breakthrough is admitting that we are not as strong as we portray ourselves to be. Your God-given opportunity is to be transparent, rejoice and tell of the good things God is doing through you, even at your weakest moments. Start being open and honest about what you can't achieve. That's when the power of God may rest on you, and you will begin to see a supernatural shift, and God will be a light unto your path.

God Still Speaks

During my time of prayer, God was speaking to me about "rain," and on this particular day, it was raining. I thank God for the season of rain that will hit your household.

> *"Then I will give you rain in due season, and the land shall yield her increase, and the trees of the field shall yield their fruit."*
> ***Leviticus 26:4***

Breakthrough Decree:

I decree that my due season is on the horizon and will cause me to receive my breakthrough. I will be fruitful and multiply. I shall be ushered into the new. I believe God is giving me a fresh pour of His anointing.

This New Launch Will Be Successful.

Nothing moves and is approved unless God speaks it (Matthew 4:4). God is working behind the scenes and turning things around for our good. So continue to pray, stay in His presence, and allow God to heal you from past hurts. Be willing to forgive, and move into the new without guilt and hurt or feeling ashamed. Remember this; God can do exceeding and abundantly above all that we ask or think. What God has in store is not even worthy to be compared to the trouble that you may have experienced in the past. Your new launch is remarkable, and the glory of God looks good on you. So be encouraged and let God deal with you from the inside out.

Day 9

Rest

- New Levels
- Rest for the journey
- God has already gone before you.
- God has prepared you for this level.
- Stay Focused
- New Assignments & New Tasks
- You're ordained to be in this season with purpose

Getting Things Accomplished

Step #1: Today, take some time to rest. Get out and do something that will help you take your mind off your circumstances. For example, I enjoy yard work, so when I'm dealing with stress or have a lot on my mind, I mow the yard and maintain the property. I am so grateful for what God has provided for me and my family. So, find what's therapeutic for you and do it.

Step #2: Spend time with family. It's needed, especially during these times. Enjoy love and laughter in the household. Take time to embrace those priceless moments. The pandemic made it hard for loved ones to be around each other, so when you get that chance to be around them, tell them you love them, celebrate them, and enjoy life.

Step #3: You're not in competition with anyone but yourself. Look at it this way; it's you versus you daily. So strive to be a better you every day.

Step #4: Speak life and encourage someone today. You never know what someone is dealing with. Set aside some meditation and prayer time. Begin to decree what you want to happen in your life and in your family's life. Prayer works!

Step #5: Take a bike ride and enjoy the scenery. Finding therapeutic things will develop peace in our life. Again, developing good habits is an important part of attaining a breakthrough.

> *"It's us against us; we're not in competition with anyone but ourselves."*
> **Prophetess Patina Winston**

Prophetic Word:

- Stay focused. God has greater for you. I know you can't see it now. But there is an abundance that's going to hit you in a way you will not understand. So stay the course and continue to walk in faith.

Your New Assignment

Whatever God needs of you, just go. You may not see it or even know it, but your new assignment is self-care first, then heal so that you may minister well and not out of a place of unforgiveness, brokenness, jealousy, and anything else that may be hiding from within. Listen, God sees you, and you're not in competition with anyone.

Matthew 11:28-30

28 Come unto me, all ye that labour and are heavy laden, and I will give you rest.

29 Take my yoke upon you, and learn of me; for I am meek and lowly in heart: and ye shall find rest unto your souls.

30 For my yoke is easy, and my burden is light.

Words of Encouragement:

You are ordained to be in this season.

God spoke you into this season for a reason with purpose.

Strive to be a better you each day

Day 10

New Launch

- God has shifted the time up
- The Ruach of God has ushered us into a new season
- Time of acceleration

New Wine Skins

Wow, we are indeed in a new space and season with a new mindset and new vision. The breath of God has shifted us into this predestined place. I want to encourage you to walk boldly in this season, knowing that God is with you. Be confident in the Lord God Almighty because He has placed something in you that is more precious than silver or gold. Guard and cherish it and show God you care about what He has given you. Times are changing. We are living in a time of acceleration; look around and see. The world we must operate in today is not the same as I remember from my childhood. God is calling us to elevate!

Take time in prayer today to commune with God. Instead of having a list of things to pray about, sit and listen. He will give you fresh revelation, knowledge, and understanding about your newness and how to walk in it and be a light while being you. Remember, God loves you, and He's adjusting your ability to hear.

Algorithm

I noticed on my social media site certain ads kept popping up. Now to my understanding, whatever ads we see are generally from the things we have either taken an interest in and searched for or liked on a specific page. I noticed things like becoming a motivational speaker, becoming a life coach, church apps on how to design flyers, or creating your own podcast. I thought it was funny but understanding that God can speak through anything to get your attention. All along, knowing these are the things that I like to do. Listen, can I tell you that your spiritual algorithm has changed? God is adding value to you. I decree an increase will cause you to expand, and your gift will make room for you.

God has a step-by-step procedure for you to accomplish. He is a problem solver. Your prayer life is the key to getting things done and experiencing a breakthrough. For example, visualize your prayers being presented before God as incense. Prayer is your tool, prayer is your algorithm, prayer is your weapon, your communication, and it sets the tone. As you begin to decree the Word of the Lord out of your mouth, you will see the manifestation of His Word. You will see the algorithm of your prayers based on how consistent you are.

Prayer

Father, I thank you for this new season and time that I am in. Thank you for endowing me with wisdom. Father, I ask that your Holy Spirit guide my mind to make the right daily decisions. I pray that I receive a fresh revelation and understanding of what I am called to and what I am called to do. Father, thank you for this new destination and journey ~Amen.

Breakthrough Decree:

God is going to make it good.

I am the seed of Abraham.

The promises of the Lord are "Yes and Amen."

When God writes the signature, it's good!

Day 11

Perspective

- New & Refreshing
- Faith to follow
- By faith, we must begin
- Miracles * Miracles * Miracles
- New things are on the horizon

Vision

Seeing things from a different perspective allows God to do something new and refreshing in your life and faith. Be as curious as a child would be and follow Him. God has good things in store for us. Who knows what your "new" may look like if you trust God? To be clear, obedience is not always easy, but it's required. Your next steps toward your breakthrough will require you to be obedient. Remember, God's thoughts are higher than ours, so certain things He wants us to have or do will require us to *listen, do, and move.* Proverbs 29:18 says, *18 Where there is no vision, the people perish: but he that keepeth the law, happy is he.* The miracles you will see are not by surprise, but God orchestrates them. We are indeed in that time where the just shall live by faith. Our vision must become stronger than ever to see and hear spiritually, discerning the times and how to operate within them. The time is now that you become unmovable in the things of God. I'm praying that your eyes will be opened and your heart is willing to follow. Watch for new dreams and visions to set you on your course

Testimony

Throughout my time of fasting and prayer, I've seen God change my outlook on things and take me places I wouldn't usually go and do things I wouldn't normally do, physically and spiritually. He was placing me in those areas to expand my thinking from the mindset of becoming great and not walking in fear or intimidation into becoming confident in Him. There is power in being led. I would never have moved forward if it wasn't for God. He came and spoke to me in my darkest times. He gave me a new vision and a new desire. It changed my vision of how I was treating others and how I needed to let the things of the past go.

Allow God to build and remake you from the inside out.

For I know the thoughts that I think toward you, saith the Lord, thoughts of peace, and not of evil, to give you an expected end.
Jeremiah 29:11

Words of Encouragement:

The path, the destination, and the journey. God is starting something new in your life and by faith, you must begin. You'll be amazed at what God has for you if we just trust Him. Hear his voice and follow his path. *By faith, you must begin.*

My sheep hear my voice, and I know them, and they follow me: **John 10:27**

But he said, Yea rather, blessed are they that hear the word of God, and keep it. **Luke 11:28**

Prayer,

Father, I pray that you will open my spiritual and physical eyes. Thank you for this new path you have shined your light on and for taking me places I have only imagined. Thank you for the manifestation of your promises coming forth. ~Amen

Breakthrough Decree:

I declare and decree that new things are on the horizon.

I decree that my new path will flourish.

I will see multiplication and increase.

The Lord shall open my eyes.

I receive multiple miracles, one after another.

Day 12

Renewed Strength

- God is changing the narrative
- Good reports - Good news
- God has us covered on every side
- Restoring our contents of love, joy, and peace
- The Glory
- Romans 8:31

The New Path and The New Journey

Today I thank God for renewed strength. I want to encourage you to continue to press your way through despite what it looks like or feels like. God has a plan and a destination, and you're on schedule for your breakthrough. Take time today, lift the name of the Lord in your prayer time, and allow Him to be the head of your life. God knows us better than we know ourselves, and He loves us beyond our understanding. Just know that God is always there when we can't feel His presence. God will move in such a way and intervene on your behalf, so be patient and wait on the Lord. Timing is everything.

I thank God for divine timing, revelation, and insight for the plans and decisions He has for you. Trust Him and His perfect timing. God loves when our faith elevates and becomes active. With new paths, there are discoveries that you will encounter. As you allow God to lead, you will discover how God will speak to you and confirm that He is with you to let you know you're on the right path. Look at the word journey, *"an act of traveling from one place to another."* You are transitioning from an old place and stepping into your new place. I declare that for you. And you're also going into a new place in Christ. So, take time to evaluate your journey and enjoy your *new one.*

Thy word is a lamp unto my feet, and a light unto my path. **Psalms 119:105**

But they that wait upon the Lord shall renew their strength; they shall mount up with wings as eagles; they shall run, and not be weary; and they shall walk, and not faint. **Isaiah 40:31**

The Shift

Be intentional in prayer. Go in with a mindset of just wanting to hear from the King. It is important to have a relationship with the Lord. Come into prayer empty and with a posture of wanting to be in God's presence. We can make all the declarations and all the decrees, but it means nothing if our heart is not in the correct posture. Make your relationship personal. We should ask for forgiveness daily about the poor choices we've made. Repenting is a prerequisite. It's a must-do. Ask God to create a clean heart and renew the right spirit within you daily. So you can have fresh ears and eyes to operate throughout your day. Be intentional. Walk in faith and watch things shift before your eyes.

Restoration Health Tips:

I'm praying that God is restoring your contents of love, joy, peace, and laughter. Laughter is good for the soul. Connect with some friends that have your best interest at heart and enjoy being in a healthy environment. Think good thoughts today. Be creative and do things that inspire you.

<u>Breakthrough Decree:</u>

I decree that I am focused on the assignment.

I decree that resources are finding me for my assignment to help me complete them and to be prosperous.

I declare and decree new healthy habits that will revive me; mentally, physically, and spiritually.

Now the God of hope fill you with all joy and peace in believing, that ye may abound in hope, through the power of the Holy Ghost.
Romans 15:13

Prayer,

Lord, I thank you for this ordained point in my breakthrough. Thank you, Father, for helping me to develop good habits that will cause me to be healthier and happier. Thank you for providing a support group that will ignite and encourage me along the way. Thank you for creating a judgment-free zone with like-minded people that are striving for the same goals. Father, I thank you for renewing my strength and giving me the energy to achieve the ability to make healthier decisions. Allow the Holy Spirit to take my mind into new places. Restore and revive me, God. ~Amen

"But he answered and said, It is written, Man shall not live by bread alone, but by every word that proceedeth out of the mouth of God."
Matthew 4:4

Day 13

Self - Control

- Not putting energy into negative things
- Negative things will drain your energy
- When people say or do things intentionally
- Why do people hinder the seed of growth?

Displaying the Fruit of the Spirit

Self-control is one fruit that we must adjust daily. Putting energy into negative thoughts or things will drain your creativity and delay what God has in store for you. Self-control is something we all should consistently embrace. The question is, how determined are you to see the best you? Be grateful for the small steps and celebrate them when you can recognize improvement. Life is a journey. You will get better with time and wisdom.

The path that God has you on is essential. *Jeremiah 29:11 says, For I know the thoughts that I think toward you, saith the Lord, thoughts of peace, and not of evil, to give you an expected end. Thoughts of peace, and not of evil.* Don't let your peace be entangled with negative narratives when God has already declared what His thoughts are towards you. God is working behind the scenes to bring you into a place of growth. Be patient and go through the steps that He has ordained for you to become the best you.

You don't have to fight this battle. God is grooming and allowing you to go through things so that on the next level, what He's calling you to will not affect you, and you'll be able to pull someone else up by your testimony of how God did it for you. Remember, God can do more for us than we can for ourselves.

Moving Forward

A major key to your breakthrough is moving forward. Of course, it's easier said than done, right? I get it. But we all need time to heal. Heal from disappointments, so-called relationships, our past, or trauma. Healing has no time frame, but I encourage you to *Get Up* and move forward. Don't allow the world's opinions to keep you from stepping into your purpose. We all come from different walks of life, and I'm no better than you, but I believe your heart has a desire to move forward.

Transparent Moment: I was in a mental place of just being tired of doing what I was doing and living how I was living. I was utterly fed up and disappointed with myself. Let me encourage you here; *that is when God can use you*. Because now your heart is ready to receive. My yes became genuine, and it was perfect timing for God to come into my life and begin to shake things up and deal with me, my character, and my integrity.

Trust in the LORD with all thine heart; and lean not unto thine own understanding. In all thy ways acknowledge him, and he shall direct thy paths. **Proverbs 3:5-6**

Galatians 5:22-23

22 But the fruit of the Spirit is love, joy, peace, longsuffering, gentleness, goodness, faith,

23 Meekness, temperance: against such there is no law.

Words of Encouragement

Ask the Lord to continue to work on you in your prayer time. But be determined to be who God called you to be, with fire and zeal. Then, you can do the things that God has declared, and you can obtain the things that are rightfully yours.

Day 14

Scriptures For Release of Burdens

Matthew 11:28-30 NLT
28 Then Jesus said, "Come to me, all of you who are weary and carry heavy burdens, and I will give you rest. 29 Take my yoke upon you. Let me teach you, because I am humble and gentle at heart, and you will find rest for your souls. 30 For my yoke is easy to bear, and the burden I give you is light."

Psalms 55:22 KJV

Cast thy burden upon the Lord, and he shall sustain thee: he shall never suffer the righteous to be moved.

Galatians 6:2 KJV

Bear ye one another's burdens, and so fulfill the law of Christ.

1 Corinthians 10:13 NLT

The temptations in your life are no different from what others experience. And God is faithful. He will not allow the temptation to be more than you can stand. When you are tempted, he will show you a way out so that you can endure.

Romans 8:15 KJV

For ye have not received the spirit of bondage again to fear; but ye have received the Spirit of adoption, whereby we cry, Abba, Father.

1 Peter 5:6-7 KJV

6 Humble yourselves therefore under the mighty hand of God, that he may exalt you in due time: 7 Casting all your care upon him; for he careth for you.

John 16:33 CSB
I have told you these things so that in me you may have peace. You will have suffering in this world. Be courageous! I have conquered the world."

Acts 20:35 KJV
I have shewed you all things, how that so laboring ye ought to support the weak, and to remember the words of the Lord Jesus, how he said, It is more blessed to give than to receive.

Hebrews 12:1 KJV
12 Wherefore seeing we also are compassed about with so great a cloud of witnesses, let us lay aside every weight, and the sin which doth so easily beset us, and let us run with patience the race that is set before us,

1 Peter 3:18 KJV
For Christ also hath once suffered for sins, the just for the unjust, that he might bring us to God, being put to death in the flesh, but quickened by the Spirit:

John 7:17 KJV
If any man will do his will, he shall know of the doctrine, whether it be of God, or whether I

speak of myself.

Psalms 145:14 CSB
The Lord helps all who fall; he raises up all who are oppressed

Acts 2:38 KJV
Then Peter said unto them, Repent, and be baptized every one of you in the name of Jesus Christ for the remission of sins, and ye shall receive the gift of the Holy Ghost.

<u>*Prophetic Word*</u>:

- In prayer, I heard, "Signed, sealed, and delivered."

God Will Always Be Victorious in Our Lives

Thank God in advance that it shall be evident that God is with us and He is for us. There is no name that is above The Lord Jesus Christ. He is the author and finisher of our faith. He is Alpha and Omega, the beginning and the end. We give Him the praise and the glory for the Holy Spirit leading and guiding us on our paths today. We thank God for the ministering angels that are dispatched around us. Lord, we just thank you for doing great and mighty things.

What shall we then say to these things? If God be for us, who can be against us? **Roman 8:31**

<u>Breakthrough Decree:</u>

I decree and declare victory today.

I decree and declare that today will be full of promise,

Full of favor,

Full of blessings,

Full of joy,

Full of health,

Full of victories,

Full of creativity,

Full of strategies so that I may walk boldly into my new. God is leading me into a place of rest and peace so that I can witness the fullness of His promise.

Day 15

Be Bold In Prayer

- Be bold in God
- Faith
- A consistent prayer life
- 2 Timothy 1:7-8
- Tell your testimony
- Freedom to move forward
- New habits

Being Bold in Prayer

Can you pray your way through? Your faith was designed to move things. When faith and prayer connect, it is powerful. So I want to encourage you today to diligently seek after God. Seek after Him wholeheartedly with zeal and with expectation. The Word says that He rewards those who earnestly seek Him.

Hebrews 11:6
But without faith, it is impossible to please him: for he that cometh to God must believe that he is and that he is a rewarder of them that diligently seek him.

Jeremiah 29:13
And ye shall seek me, and find me, when ye shall search for me with all your heart.

Prayer is simply communication with the Father. Talking with Him daily like you would call up one of your best friends, or even one of your family members, or one of your home boys or home girls and pour out to them the concerns of your heart and talk about things that are going on in your life. The Father also wants that same energy and line of communication extended to him. He desires to hear from you.

The Bible tells us in Hebrews 4:16 to come boldly to the throne of grace so that we may obtain mercy and find grace to help in the time of need. Developing a good habit of putting Him first before going to social media sites to rant. Frequently those very things that we trust or the people that we trust in will let you down every time, and what you have trusted them with and discussed in private now becomes gossip. So, we must be careful and mindful of the things and people we put before God instead of seeking Him first. The answer and the solution to whatever you may be going through will be found in Him.

New Habits

The only way up is down. What do I mean by that? I'm glad you asked. The only way up is to develop a consistent prayer life even when you don't feel like getting up before your workday or taking time on your lunch break; finding the time is all that matters. We must do this. Breaking old habits takes time and consistency, while pressing your way to your breakthrough will be found in your determination. How determined are you to let go of old habits?

Freedom to Move Forward

The transition out of the old and into the new will forever change your perspective on the things that matter the most. Fear, doubt, and anxiety will be a thing of the past when you begin to take the necessary steps toward change. The Bible tells us in *2 Timothy 1:7 God did not give us the spirit of fear; but of power, and love, and of a sound mind.* Those three steps are major keys to your breakthrough; power, love, and a sound mind. Faith over fear. The keys have been handed to us. Now it's up to us to move accordingly. Whom the Son set free is free indeed (John 8:36). This is your fresh start.

The Power to Decree a Thing

Job 22:28 28
Thou shalt also decree a thing, and it shall be established unto thee: and the light shall shine upon thy ways.

Testimony

As you begin to move forward, share your testimony with others because your voice matters. It's amazing when we can tell other people how amazing God is. Some may not understand, but they will be curious enough to say, "How did you do it?"

So continue to be a light, and let God do the rest. Your breakthrough is BIG, and others around you will notice that God is up to something BIG.

Day 16

Open Doors

- Invitation
- Command your seed
- Sow in faith
- New territory - New Tent
- God has prepared you
- Victory in the Lord will be in his power
- Ephesians 6:10 - Finally, my brethren, be strong in the Lord, and in the power of his might

Seeds of Expectation

Look for the open door. There will be an unexpected invitation for you to come up higher.

You have been praying and waiting with great expectation. Watch for the seeds of patience, good works, commitment, and prayer to produce. This is your door of promotion. Don't hesitate to move forward in faith. God will give you the things to say crossing over into your due season. Do not allow fear of leaders to intimidate you. Just know that you are ordained to be in this place. I call it the right place at the right time, blessings. Locking arms with like-minded people will inspire and encourage the gift and the plans of God. Continue to listen for new instructions and new assignments. Pray and ask God to give you directions to help you navigate this new territory. *Prayer is your key*. Use it to unlock your new season and your ability to hear and navigate well.

Instructions:

Get a planner and visually map out the things that God has given. Doing this will help you stay focused and on track. Seeing this will help you navigate and begin to get in sync with God's timing.

Testimony

You will be among great leaders; I was called to a platform on social media to speak and didn't know that I would receive a prophetic word while attending. The man of God came on and prophesied to me about new territory and a new tent. He went on to say that victory will be in the Lord; not by might, not by power but by his spirit and ridiculous favor was going to be in this season. Now mind you, I'm going through. But I was still expecting what God was getting ready to do in my life while having a heart of gratefulness. I want to challenge you to command your seed, be patient, and let patience work her perfect peace. God's timing is unmatched. Things can turn in your favor instantly, and that's what God did for me. I shifted into a new season of liberty and freedom.

Breakthrough Decree:

I decree that my seed will flourish in this season in the mighty name of Jesus.

Romans 8:19
For the earnest expectation of the creation eagerly waits for the revealing of the sons of God.

Ephesians 3:20

Now unto him that is able to do exceeding abundantly above all that we ask or think, according to the power that worketh in us

Prophetic Word:

- God has orchestrated something grand on your behalf, so walk in it with power and authority, keeping God in the forefront. God has prepared you for this appointed place. Celebrate your growth and maturity. Only you know what you've been through and what it took to get to this point. I decree that favor from the north, south, east, and west will be your portion in this season. Favor with resources, favor with finances, and favor with man. I decree that like-minded people will pour into you on your new journey

Day 17

Sow

Lord Let the Seed Produce

The definition of *sow* in the Merriam-Webster dictionary is to plant seed for growth, especially by scattering, to set something in motion, begin an enterprise. So today, my prayer is Lord, let the seed produce; not only let it produce but allow it to multiply and be fruitful. What can you sow that will set your seed in motion? Ask God to reveal what you need to sow and where to sow.

Luke 6:38

Give, and it will be given to you. A good measure, pressed down, shaken together and running over, will be poured into your lap. For with the measure you use, it will be measured to you."

The Benefits of Sowing

I'm praying that my testimony will bless you. I can only pour out what's in me. These same principles I'm sharing with you have blessed me in more ways than one. Let me share this with you. I used to hate tithing. I was always a giver but only saw increments of what could be. Then, God began to use my wife to minister to me on how to reach the fullness of being blessed.

I was in debt and couldn't see myself getting out. Credit cards maxed out, truck due, and the primary bills it takes to keep a house running. All while trying to be a provider for my family. I was always behind until I noticed my wife getting promotions left and right on her job, in ministry and in her finances. Her credit score was going up rapidly. Favor with random people just coming to bless her for being her unique self. A very special lady now close to us came up and just blessed her, saying, "God said to bless you."

Can you imagine how in awe I was? I'm like, "God, what am I doing wrong?"

After seeing things move rapidly for my wife, I sat down with my wife and began to ask her what am I missing? I was mentally and physically drained at my lowest point, and everything I tried wasn't working. We sat down, and she said, "Baby, I've been tithing for a whole year, and I've been intentionally sowing into other people." That was it for me. I had to follow suit. Listen, things changed in our lives rapidly when we got on the same page.

A major key is yielding unto the Lord. Your devotion to Him is very important. My approach became different, and my eyes were opened once I stepped back. Yielding what you have, your gifts, your time, and your tenth is also an act of obedience and worship. It's ok. Trust God. Who knows us better? Stay consistent and stick with it. God is not a slot machine, but His Word is rich and alive, and it's true and full of power. It's our very well-being. God's love will always win.

Prayer,

Father God, in the mighty name of Jesus Christ, I thank you for doing something bright, new, and exciting. Father, I thank you for a new outlook, a new day, and a fresh start. Father, I ask that you forgive me of my sin, create a clean heart, and renew a right spirit within me. Father, I thank you for giving me power, authority, and dominion to command the seed to prosper, grow to be fruitful, and multiply. Father, thank you for showing me that there is power in my words. I command the seed to grow and to go forth to produce and to manifest. Lord, I thank you for this path and the intimate time with you drawing me closer to you. ~Amen

Prophetic Word:

- Sow the change that you want to see come forward in your life.

- Don't worry about it God's got it.

Day 18

Great Things Are on the Horizon

- Deuteronomy 28:12
- Jeremiah 29:11

Supernatural Shift

It's going to rain, and there is an abundance of it. God is raining on your seed. This new season Father, I thank you for blessing our hands. I thank you, Lord, for the latter rain being greater than the former rain. Father, I thank you for giving us hope and a future; your plan is to prosper us. Thank you for giving us the mindset to be creative and giving us the space and capacity to create new ideas for the kingdom for your glory. Father, thank you for the pouring of your spirit so that we may be able to receive fresh revelation and knowledge on how to function in these times. Father, give us an ear to hear and be receptive to your words. Surround us with people that are like-minded and inspired to move forward. Father, we thank you for the countenance of joy being restored and the burdens being lifted. Father God, thank you for being the breaker and going before us. God, we thank you for making the impossible possible and allowing us to walk into the supernatural.

Words of Encouragement:

I'm excited about your breakthrough. I'm praying that God will continue to shine his light on your path. Remember, you have a cloud of witnesses cheering you on. You got this!

Prophetic Word:

- Forgiveness will cause your water to break

- Forgiveness is the key to moving forward

Day 19

Breakthrough

- Advance
- Increase
- God is doing great and mighty things

Breakthrough

You are in the midst of a supernatural shift. This shift will be solely God ushering you into a new place. Merriam-Webster Dictionary defines *breakthrough* as a sudden increase in knowledge and understanding, an important discovery that happens after trying to understand or explain something for a long time. Similar words to describe breakthrough are advancement, enhancement, improvement, and refinement. I was led to look up the word breakthrough and was amazed at what I found. I believe we are about to witness a great move of God in this hour. And it will start from the inside and work its way outward. The timing of this is profound.

God has been speaking a lot about the seed and the multiple blessings within one small seed. We must become great stewards of the seeds God has allowed us to partake of because it's attached to our purpose. Look at this scripture in 1 Corinthians 3:6-9, *I have planted, Apollos watered; but God gave the increase.* We must remember that whenever there is an increase, know that God allowed it. It's a time to be grateful and appreciative of what God is doing, even if we cannot see it yet. Great and mighty things I declare to you shall be your portion. Things undeserved, but His love can reach far enough to elevate you wherever you are. God's love is drawing us near, and He is sealing things on your behalf.

Breakthrough Decree:

I decree that I will see an increase in my family, my finances, my career path, my health and the area of entrepreneurship, and business relationships that will help position me.

Prayer of Gratitude

Father God, I bless you today in the mighty name of Jesus. I thank you for sitting high and looking low. Father, forgive me of my sins and remove anything that is not of you. Create a clean heart and renew the right spirit within me so I may get it right today, God. Father, I thank you for this shift. I thank you for the supernatural taking place. I bless you, Lord, for doing great and mighty things. Thank you for your hand being strong and mighty. I also thank you for your glory, Lord. You said where we are weak, you are strong, so I thank you, Lord, for refreshing us in you. In Jesus' mighty name. ~Amen

Words Of Encouragement

The race is not given to the swift nor the strong but to the one who will endure until the end. Continue to press towards the mark of the high calling until you see your breakthrough. *1 Corinthians 2:9 But as it is written, Eye hath not seen, nor ear heard, neither have entered into the heart of man, the things which God hath prepared for them that love him.*

Day 20

The Path

- Psalms 91:1 KJV
- Psalms 90:1

Words of Encouragement

    Great and mighty is our God. A lot of good things are going on, and it's refreshing and needed, so be encouraged and know that you're headed in the right direction. The push was necessary. I believe that this season, God calls you to move forward confidently and without hesitation. Faith will cause you to blossom in this season of breakthrough. You have been given new power and authority because of your yes to the Lord. Doors are going to open for you far beyond your understanding. You will have favor with God and with man so be in expectation and continue to look for the manifestation of the Word. Keep the excitement and stay the course. Be bold in the Lord and continue to pray. What God is getting ready to do for you will be mind-blowing. Unexpected gifts will greet you as you enter the dwelling place.

Lord, you have been our dwelling place throughout all generations. **Psalms 90:1**

He that dwelleth in the secret place of the most High shall abide under the shadow of the Almighty.
Psalms 91:1

Breakthrough Decrees:

I will abide in Him.

When God blesses me, I am going to have wow moments.

The Dwelling Place

When I think about the dwelling place, I think about a safe, secret place of refuge, having the confidence of knowing that God is covering me. The intimate space and time with the Father allows Him to come in and do something new within you as you draw near Him. It's a place where renewed strength resides. The dwelling place will revive you and give you hope to continue and press forward into your purpose. The Holy Spirit gives fresh revelation, understanding, and instructions to navigate you to your breakthrough this season. This is where God will reveal His mysteries to us when we enter the dwelling place.

The Lord shall be your confidence. No longer will you walk in fear or doubt. Those days are behind you because you have experienced the hand of God. You will walk in the fullness of your true identity and who God called you to be. In the dwelling place, you will flourish in health and prosperity. God will restore you, and what's attached to you will increase.

Prayer,

Father, I thank you for the shift. Thank you for allowing me to be ahead of the shift. Thank you, Lord, for speaking to me and giving me revelation on the things to come and how to prepare ahead of time. Father, thank you for revealing who I am in you and revealing my identity to me. Thank you for the dwelling place. Father, thank you for providing a place of refuge and safety for me. You are more than enough. ~Amen

Day 21

Dwell

Dwell	Go with
Live In	Correspond
Specified place	Brooks
To remain	To keep
Time	Attention
To live as Resident	Agree
Nest	Be connected with
Inhabit	Attached to
Exist	To speak
Living	To write
Present	Agree
Obtain	Harmonize

This is an interesting study of words connected to the word dwell. When doing this study, you will find that this is speaking on the attributes of God. It's amazing how one word says a lot about our Heavenly Father. God is calling us to dwell in Him. This is the safest place to be. There is no other place like living under the blessing of God and flowing in His glory. I want to declare that the peace, freedom, and joy you have been searching for are in the dwelling place. Allow the Holy Spirit to be your GPS and allow Him to navigate to you the location of the dwelling place.

Listen, we've all lived a life of toil, hurt, shame, and brokenness, but I have to encourage you and let you know that you don't have to live like that anymore and that you can break through that mindset. The Father is waiting to receive us all with open arms.

I prophesy to you today to (GET UP) lift your head up and live in the abundance that Jesus said is rightfully yours. Taking the first step is never easy but just know you are not doing it alone. Remember *Jeremiah 29:11 For I know the plans I have for you," declares the Lord, "plans to prosper you and not to harm you, plans to give you hope and a future.*

Be encouraged; you have a bright future ahead of you!

Listen prophetically, let the glory be your place of residence, dwell in the safe place, and live under His shadow. His provision is beyond our understanding. I believe God is calling us to dwell in this place. You deserve it and don't be discouraged by your story. My writing coach always tells us that we matter and our testimony is important. Your story will help others overcome what you have already faced. This is your set time. You got this! Be confident, and most importantly, take the time to glorify God for your breakthrough.

4 Abide in me, and I in you. As the branch cannot bear fruit of itself, except it abide in the vine; no more can ye, except ye abide in me.

5 I am the vine, ye are the branches: He that abideth in me, and I in him, the same bringeth forth much fruit: for without me ye can do nothing. **John 15:4-5**

1 He that dwelleth in the secret place of the most High shall abide under the shadow of the Almighty.

2 I will say of the Lord, He is my refuge and my fortress: my God; in him will I trust. **Psalms 91:1-2**

Thanking God for the Dwelling Place

It's important to allow God to come into your life. The invitation for the Most High God to come in is an indication of surrendering. Surrendering to God will open so many things up for you. Because, to be honest, "we" think we know the way. In actuality, "we" don't even have a clue. Surrendering is also a sign of allowing God to lead. So often, "we" can get in the way of God's plan and try to rush things out of His timing and not fully understand why he is taking us through specific routes.

I encourage you today to pay attention to the routes and ask for understanding so that you may make decisions based on what He is showing you and apply wisdom.

There is also an awakening that will take place in the dwelling place. God will begin to reveal certain things that He wants you to see or know. It's awesome that He still wants to be intimate with us. Take a moment and give God some praise and meditate on his goodness.

Prayer,

Father, thank you for blessing me, exceeding, abundantly above all that I could ask or think. Father, forgive me of my sins. Anything that is not like you, I ask that you remove it. Create in me a clean heart and renew a right spirit within me. Father God, thank you for meeting me in the dwelling place.

Thank you for preparing this place for our families to dwell in. Father, thank you for the glory surrounding us in this place. You deserve the honor. I am grateful to be able to abide in you and bare the same fruit. Father, thank you for the call to be intimate with you in this time of prayer to receive fresh revelation and get understanding and knowledge.

Father, thank you for the breakthrough season and for being the breaker who goes before us and makes all paths straight.

Thank you for interceding on our behalf and speaking things into existence. Matthew 4:4 "But he answered and said, It is written, Man shall not live by bread alone, but by every word that proceedeth out of the mouth of God."

Father, thank you for everything proceeding out of your mouth, our growth, your glory, the dwelling place you have called for us to be in, and it's all by you speaking it. I don't take it lightly. Oh God, we thank you for choosing us. Continue to endow us with resources, information, creativity, and new strategies for this season that we are entering. You know what we need to be equipped with and the things that are ahead of us.

Father, thank you for your Word being quick, and I glorify your name, Lord. Father, you said you watch over your Word to perform it, and it's evident in what you're doing right now and the direction you want us to go in.
~Amen

Words of Encouragement

God is changing your narrative, character, countenance, sound, prayer, trajectory, steps, surroundings, income, finances, health, and wealth in the dwelling place.

Prophetic Word:

- The glory shall be your place of residence in this season.
- The glory shall be a barrier and fortress of protection.

Testimony

God Shall Reveal

I'm praying that God has met you on your quest to breakthrough. I want to share a testimony to further encourage you so you can expect what God has in store for you. My wife and I decided to take a ride to find a desk for our office, and I just couldn't stop thinking about the prophetic word that was given to me about "God shall reveal" from a good friend of ours that flows heavily in the prophetic. On our ride, we were talking and catching up on some much-needed time together; while laughing, I received a notification from my email. My wife gave me that look like, "Husband, you better not answer that email," so I didn't. As we continued down the road, we listened to one of our favorite gospel radio stations, and we were enjoying the word that was going forth and playing some music on our way to her favorite store. Then, out of nowhere, a second notification came to my phone.

Now this email is very important because it was the very thing my wife and I had been praying about during our time of fasting. Now listen, just the night before, a little before midnight, my wife and I were preparing and getting things in order that needed to be turned in. God ushered us into what He wanted us to do at that very moment. Before the email even hit my inbox we were already acting on what was requested, God revealed specific directions to us that allowed us to be ahead of it. I began to tell my wife this is weird. What came to my mind was Paul and Silas in *Acts 16:25-26 About midnight Paul and Silas were praying and singing hymns to God, and the other prisoners were listening to them. 26 Suddenly there was such a violent earthquake that the foundations of the prison were shaken. At once all the prison doors flew open, and everyone's chains came loose.*

I got stirred up during the car ride because I caught the revelation. God has broken the chains off of us and freed us from the things that were keeping us bound. God heard our prayers. He heard our petition before Him, and He answered supernaturally. We were in complete awe sitting in the car and excited about what God was getting ready to do in the next chapter of our lives. Now, this is all driven by the Holy Spirit and divine timing. I want to take a minute to encourage you. It is important that you pray and be on one accord before making a major decision. God gave us intel that we could not find in past times, and it was revealed at the very moment of inviting the Lord into our decision-making.

God revealed the very thing that became a primary key to our breakthrough. Acknowledge God in all your ways, and He will direct your path. Keep this in mind: I have been fasting and praying for twenty-one days, and what God revealed to me was Daniel. After fasting and praying for twenty-one days, answered prayers were released and revealed.

Daniel 10:12-13

Then said he unto me, Fear not, Daniel: for from the first day that thou didst set thine heart to understand, and to chasten thyself before thy God, thy words were heard, and I am come for thy words.

13 But the prince of the kingdom of Persia withstood me one and twenty days: but, lo, Michael, one of the chief princes, came to help me; and I remained there with the kings of Persia.

Answered Prayers

It took the angel twenty-one days to break through to get the message to Daniel. And here I am the day after the fast day twenty-two, we received a spiritual key to unlocking our breakthrough. This key destroyed strongholds and generational curses and took our faith to a new dimension. I decree that this will be the best season of your life. Momentum and acceleration will shift in your favor.

Prophetic Words:

- Be open to what God wants to do in your life.

- God is moving supernaturally in this hour.

- You just stepped into divine timing. You are operating in a different time zone.

- Your best season is ahead of you. Lord, send the rain. The increase is in the forecast.

- Multiplication and plenty shall be your portion. Allow God to position you to reign.

- God's love will shine through every dark place. Abide in love; a new love will be birthed out of you. God is real and his angels are real too.

- Soar.

Words of Encouragement:

Continue to meditate, pray and watch God do it.

Revealed: To make it known through divine inspiration.

Keep your eyes open spiritually and physically.

You're already victorious.

The battle is not ours, but it's the Lords.

You have won already.

Welcome to your new season.

Breakthrough Decrees

- You are more than a conqueror.
- I decree that I will see multiple victories.
- I declare and decree that I will flourish.
- Increase is my portion.
- I declare that it shall happen suddenly.
- I declare and decree an uninterrupted flow shall manifest.
- The glory shall be my place of residence in this season.
- I declare and decree that I am walking on new ground and territory.
- I decree a spiritual awakening.
- I declare and decree that my prayer life will go to new levels.
- I decree that my faith will speak for me.

- I decree that I am the head and not the tail.
- I declare divine speed to accomplish what God spoke over me.
- I decree that this is my season.
- I declare a prophetic rain will shift me into abundance.

May God continue to increase in you, as you apply those keys that will help unlock your breakthrough.

LAWRENCE WINSTON

Family Picture

Names from left to right:
Back Row: Tiana Winston, Rubie Adams, Lawrence Winston,
Patina Winston, Annette Bryant
Second Row: Yael Winston, Evan Winston, Gabrielle Winston
Front Row: Jazarria Winston

www.ingramcontent.com/pod-product-compliance
Lightning Source LLC
Chambersburg PA
CBHW071133090426
42736CB00012B/2113